BE STRONG!!!

The Lord is always with you

BE STRONG!!!

The Lord is always with you

Vivienne Caldwell

ARPress
ILLUMINATING IDEAS
EMPOWERING VOICES

ARPress
45 Dan Road Suite 5
Canton MA 02021
Hotline: 1(888) 821-0229
Fax: 1(508) 545-7580

Ordering Information:
Quantity sales. Special discounts are available on quantity purchases by corporations, associations, and others. For details, contact the publisher at the address above.

ISBN-13:   Paperback   979-8-89356-871-4
                eBook   979-8-89356-872-1

Library of Congress Control Number: 2024909125

Table of Contents

My Testimony

I was verbally and physically abused and still suffer resentment. I was in a very toxic marriage and growing up, seeing my parents going through a very brutal marriage. At the age of 5, I was sent to the country to live with my aunt who verbally and physically abused me. When I was 19 years of age, I accepted Jesus Christ as my Lord and Savior and I realized that forgiveness is essential in recovering self-worth. I have to learn to value myself enough to say to the one who hurt me, "What you think of me doesn't define me, what you do to me won't destroy me. I'm choosing to let this go so I can be free of all toxicity."

This inspired me not to hope for a better future, but to pursue one, making use of the untapped talents that had been suffocated by self-belittlement and fear of criticism.

I needed to make time for the Lord. If I just learn to slow down, break away from my hectic schedules and be okay with silence, God will have his chance to speak.

Lord, you are my source, and I draw from you the capacity to be kind. I draw from you the forgiveness I need to extend right now. I draw from you the love I need to express.

Lord, this is painful, and I do not like it. But I choose to submit to you because you are trustworthy and loving. I am willing to persevere until you accomplish in me whatever you want. I choose to draw from your strength for everything I need.

Life can be tough when facing difficulties, obstacles or in a crisis moment. Life has its ups and downs, but it does not mean that worst time will remain forever. Sometimes you must face daunting challenges, failure that will smack you down to the ground, and your success story will begin when you get back up on your feet, shake the dust from your clothes and continue to have faith and trust God because He will make a way for you. Just **BE STRONG** and courageous and God will see you through because the God in the valley is the same God on the mountain top.

Chapter 1

"My brethren, count it all joy when you fall into divers' temptations, knowing this, that the trying of your faith worketh patience. But let patience have her perfect work, that you may be perfect and entire, wanting nothing."

(James 1:2-4)

Count It All Joy

How on earth can we "consider it all joy" when we face terrible hardship? Jesus proclaimed, "in this world you will have trouble" *(John 16:33)*

How then can we rejoice when we face trouble? It is through our hardships that Christ often makes himself known to us. If we lived trouble-free lives, what need would we have for a Savior? It is because we live fragile lives that we can see Jesus clearly.

When we face a problem head-on with the certainty that God will provide a solution and the strength to endure, we gain spiritual stamina. Our faith develops because of dealing with spiritual resistance.

Through the indwelling Holy Spirit, we can find the faith to rejoice in our pain.

This is possible because we not only have the assurance that God will provide, but we also can trust that when we walk with Him, we will be better prepared to face the next obstacle.

Chapter 2

Not Every Obstacle Is Meant To Be Overcome

Though we may know what God wants us to do, we can become blinded by the desire for money, possessions, or prestige. We can avoid Balaam's mistake by looking past the allure of fame or fortune to the long-range benefits of following God.

We sometimes strike out at blameless people who get in our way because we are embarrassed, or our pride is hurt. Lashing out at others can be a sign that something is wrong with us. Do not allow your own hurt pride to lead you to hurt others. Not every obstacle is meant to be overcome. Some are placed by God to keep us from doing something foolish. When our plans are hindered, we should not assume that it is Satan trying to stop us. It might be God trying to protect us.

Chapter 3

"And when Haman saw that Mordecai bowed not, nor did him reverence, then was Haman full of wrath."

(Esther Chapters 3 and 4)

Attitude Of Forgiveness

The most arrogant people are often those who must measure their self-worth by the power or influence they think they have over others. Haman was an extremely arrogant leader.

He recognized the King as his superior but could not accept anyone as an equal. When Mordecai refused to bow in submission to him, Haman wanted to destroy him. He became consumed with hatred for Mordecai. He was already filled with racial hatred for all Jewish people because of the long-standing hatred between the Jews and Haman's ancestors, the Amalekites. Mordecai's dedication to God and his refusal to give homage to any human person challenged Haman's self-centered religion.

Haman saw the Jews as a threat to his power, and he decided to kill all Jews. God was preparing Haman's downfall and the protection of his people long before Haman came to power.

Haman died on the gallows he had built to hang Mordecai, and his plan to wipe out the Jews was thwarted. Haman risked everything for an evil purpose and lost.

Our initial response to the story about Haman is to say that he got what he deserved. But the Bible leads us to ask deeper questions: "How much of Haman is in me/us?" "Do I desire to control others?" "Am I threatened when others don't appreciate me as I think they should?" "Do I want revenge when my pride is attacked?" Confess these attitudes to God and ask him to replace them with an attitude of forgiveness. Otherwise, God's Justice will settle the matter.

Chapter 4

"It was meet that we should be merry and be glad: for this thy brother was dead, and is alive again; and was lost, and is found."

(Luke 15:11-32)

God's Open Arms

The story of the prodigal son shows us fewer positive aspect of independence-one which sadly is woven into the fabric of human nature. The wayward son takes charge of his own life and shuns his father's care and protection. Fortunately, the story does not stop after revealing the boy's downward spiral of sin; it also shows us the restoring grace of God.

Sin meant acting independently of God's will. It begins with a desire that is outside his plan. Next comes a decision to act on the desire. When we do, we find ourselves like the prodigal in a "distant country" which is anywhere outside the will of God. To remain there requires deception. We deceive ourselves by thinking that we know better than God and ignoring any consequences. Defeat follows. For a time, all may seem fine, but like the reckless son in the story, we will find that our way leads to defeat.

Finally, we will arrive at despair resulting from famine of spirit, emotions, or relationships. That leads into desperation where our choices are few and distasteful. Jesus gave this account of an earthly father's forgiving love because he desired to point us to the restoring grace of our heavenly Father. God waits with open arms for us, his wandering children.

The parable of the prodigal son paints a similar picture of our heavenly Father's attitude towards us, his children, which illustrates the magnificence of Grace. In *Luke 15:20*, the one who was sinned against is running out to eagerly welcome back the one who sinned. Be sure to notice how the one who was mistreated shows compassion to the one who was at fault.

The prodigal did not know that his full rights as a son would be restored. As believers, we know in advance what awaits us when we humbly return to our heavenly father. Because of grace, we can count on acceptance no matter how long we have been absent from him or how far we have wandered.

Grace guarantees that our Lord will greet us with compassion and forgiveness, lovingly restoring us to full rights as his children. It is not good deeds or even the right words of apology that matter; it is our position in Christ. When God sees that we belong to His son, He forgives us.

The parable of the prodigal Son points us to the truth that because of Jesus Christ, we are forgiven even before we return. While this does not give us license to sin *(Rom. 6:1-2)* it does give us reason to celebrate. Our Father is waiting to welcome us home.

Chapter 5

"But when he was strong, his heart was lifted up to his destruction: for he transgressed against the Lord his God and went into the temple of the Lord to burn incense upon the altar of increase."

(2 Chronicles 25:16)

Give God The Honor

We are never closer to failure than during our greatest success. If we fail to recognize God's part in our achievements, they are no better than failures.

We owe a debt of thanksgiving to God for our very lives. If God is not getting the credit for your successes, should you not start looking at your life differently?

If God has given you wealth, influence, popularity, and power, be thankful, but be careful. God hates pride. While it is normal to feel elation when we accomplish something, it is wrong to be disdainful of God or to look down on others. Check your attitudes and remember to give God the credit for what you have. Use your gifts in ways that please Him.

No matter what your position in society, God expects you to honor, worship, and obey Him. God requires lifelong obedience. A spirit of obedience is not enough. Practice being consistent in your faith every day; that way you will build a lifelong of obedience. Otherwise, you too may become more famous for your downfall than for your success.

Chapter 6

"But Jonah rose up to flee unto Tarshish from the presence of the Lord and went down to Joppa: and he found a ship going to Tarshish: so, he paid the fare thereof, and went down into it, to go with them unto Tarshish from the presence of the Lord."

(Jonah 1:1-17)

Do Not Flee From God's Presence

Good people try to run from God in many ways and end up experiencing miseries like Jonah's while running from the Lord. The prophet overlooked some essentials that we should all keep in mind. In the first place, he incorrectly assumed that fleeing from God would release him from having to obey.

He probably never imagined how persistent the Lord can be when He calls us to a duty station. It is impossible to run from God successfully. His love will pursue us even to the depths of the sea to conform us to His will and His plan for our lives.

God simply will not be deterred by our slippery disobedience. When you run from God, there is no hiding place, even in the bottom of the sea. Our entire life is always visible to the Lord. So instead of trying to flee from His presence, welcome it.

Chapter 7

"But he himself went a day's journey into the wilderness and came and sat down under a Juniper tree: and he requested for himself that he might die; and said, it is enough; now, O Lord, take away my life; for I am not better than my fathers."

(1 Kings 19:4; Genesis 3:6; 1Kings 11;1-3)

Moments of Weakness

The eyes look, the mind desires, and the will acts. David looked at Uriah's wife, inquired about her and then he acted.

Achan who helped in the Jericho conquest noticed all the material wealth, coveted it in his mind and took what he wanted *(Joshua 7:20-21)*

In times of weakness, remember the word H. A. L. T. Not to let yourself become **Hungry**, **Angry**, **Lonely** or **Tired**. Fix your attention on the Lord, draw strength from Him, and experience victory over temptation.

Times of Temptation

We can put a "**H. A. L. T**" to letting ourselves be **Hungry**, **Angry**, **Lonely**, **Tired**. We are to be wise, to eat regularly, experience the peace God offers, stay in fellowship with others, and get enough rest.

Does God ever tempt us? No. According to *(James 1:13)*, "Our Father does not want us to do evil; He will, however, test us to reveal to you and me our motives and attitudes. Jesus also uses times of testing to mature us and transform us into Christ's likeness. His work is always for our good. It is not sinful to experience temptation. Feeling tempted is not the same as committing a sin. Only when we act upon the enticement do we cross the line into sin.

FEAR IS A REACTION. COURAGE IS A DECISION.

Chapter 8

"O Lord thou hast searched me and know me. Thou knowest my down sitting and mine uprising, thou understandest my thought afar off."

(Psalm 139:2)

God Is Everywhere

Sometimes people who try to run from God are acting out of pure selfishness. It seems we have an unlimited capacity to believe we know what is best for us, no matter what God thinks or says.

At times we hesitate out of simple fear; we are afraid that we might not succeed; we are concerned that others will be critical of our efforts; or perhaps we fear obedience might be too costly.

But no matter what our reason is, we often fail to recognize the high price of turning aside and trying to flee from the Lord. You cannot run from the Lord without inflicting heavy punishment on innocent people. You cannot leave little children fatherless or motherless without reaping lifelong pain and suffering. Nor can you sin against the Lord without paying a terrible price yourself and hurting others in the process.

Chapter 9

"The fear of the Lord is to hate evil: Pride, and arrogancy, and the evil way, and the froward mouth, do I hate."

(Proverb 8:13)

The Fear of The Lord

The fear of the Lord is something positive and healthy that is clearly defined in several different scriptures. "The Fear of the Lord is to hate evil."

God says we are to hate evil because He himself hates evil in all its forms for a simple reason – namely, the Lord sees the corrupting, destructive influences that wickedness has on us.

We often fail to see any corruption at all. In fact, we sometimes look at evil and think that it is not too bad. Satan's job is to camouflage iniquity until it appears quite innocent or even attractive. In fact, the enemy is so successful in His deception that we often fall into His snares without any guilt. That is why we must learn to view things as the Lord sees them. We need to develop such a holy hatred for evil that we shun and refuse it at every turn.

Chapter 10

What It Means to Fear God

Proper fear of the Lord produces all manner of fruit in the Christian's life. It leads to our hating evil as God does and it is also the beginning of wisdom. The more we acquire divine understanding the greater will be our love for the scriptures and the Lord's commandments.

God-fearing people also find that "light arises in the darkness for the upright". This does not mean that we will never have painful situations or periods of distress in the valley – we will still have trials, headaches, and tears, like the rest of mankind. But in our hardships, we are promised the light of deliverance.

The Bible says that "the angel of the Lord encamps around those who fear Him and rescues them" *(Psalm 34:7)*. We who believes will be surrounded so that nothing can get at us without divine permission.

Chapter 11

"Wherefore comfort yourselves together, and edify one another, even as also you do."

(1 Thessalonians 5:11)

Encourage Each Other

Paul gives many specific examples of how we can encourage others:

5:11 - Build each other up. Point out to someone a quality you appreciate in him or her.

5:12 - Respect leaders. Look for ways to cooperate

5:13 – Hold leaders in highest regard. Hold back your critical comments about those in positions of responsibility. Say "thank you" to your leaders for their efforts.

5:13 – Live in peace. Search for ways to get along with others

5:14 – Warn the idle. Challenge someone to join you in a project

5:14 – Encourage the timid. Encourage those who are timid by reminding them of God's promise.

5:14 – Help the weak. Support those who are weak by loving them and praying for them

5:14 – Be patient. Think of a situation that tries your patience, and plan ahead of time how you can stay calm.

5:15 – Resist revenge. Instead of planning to get even with those who mistreat you, do good to them.

5:16 – Be joyful. Remember that even during turmoil, God is in control

5:17 – Pray continually. God is always with you – Talk to Him.

5:18 – Give thanks. Make a list of all the gifts God has given you, giving thanks to God for each one.

5:19 – Do not put out the Spirit's fire. Cooperate with the spirit the next time He prompts you to participate in a Christian meeting.

5:20 – Do not treat prophecies with contempt. Receive God's word from those who speak for him.

5:22 – Avoid every kind of evil. Avoid situations where you will be drawn into temptation.

5:23 – Count on God's constant help. Realize that the Christian life is to be lived not in our own strength but through God's power.

Chapter 12

"Bless the Lord, O my soul: and all that is within me, bless his holy name."

(Psalm 103:1)

God's Love for Us

Benefits God Showers on us in Love

- He forgives our sin *(103:3)*

- Satisfies us with good things *(103:5)*

- Executes righteousness and justice *(103:6)*

- He is slow to anger and abounds in mercy *(103:8)*

- He does not deal with us as our sins deserve *(103:10)*

- He has removed our sin as far as the East is from the West

(103:12)

He has not forgotten us. The death of Christ is the measure of God's love for you.

Chapter 13

"I will bless the Lord at all times: his praise shall continually be in my mouth."

(Psalm 34:1)

Great Blessings

God promises great blessings to his people, but many of these blessings require active participation.

- He will deliver us from fear *(34:4)*

- Save us out of our troubles *(34:6)*

- Guard and deliver us *(34:7)*

- Show us goodness *(34:8)*

- Supply our needs *(34:9)*

- Listen when we talk to Him *(34:15)*

- Redeem us *(34:22)*

But we must do our part. We can expect His blessings when we:

- Seek Him *(34:4)*

- Cry out to Him *(34:6)*

- Trust Him *(34:8)*

- Fear Him *(34:7,9)*

- Refrain from lying *(34:13)*

- Turn from evil, do good and seek peace *(34:14)*

- Are humble *(34:18)*

- Serve Him *(34:22)*

Chapter 14

"That he may incline our hearts unto him, to walk in all his ways, and to keep his commandments, and his statutes, and his judgments, which he commanded our fathers."

(1 Kings 8:58)

Solomon's Five Basic Requests

Solomon praised the Lord and prayed for the people. His prayer can be a pattern for our prayers. He had five basic requests:

- For God's presence *(8:57)*

- For the desire to do God's will in everything (turn our hearts to Him) *(8:58)*

- For help with each day's needs. *(8:59)*

- For the desire and ability to obey God's decrees and commands *(8:58)*

- For the spread of God's kingdom to the entire world *(8:60)*

So, when Solomon went to Gibeon, he sought God and found Him. When Solomon started a project, it was for the purpose of the presence of God. When Solomon finished the project, he prayed God's continual presence. One of the worst crimes people commit against God is failing to praise Him with a heart of gratitude.

Chapter 15

"God of my righteousness: thou hast enlarged me when I was in distress; have mercy upon me and hear my prayer.

(Psalm 4:11)

Spirit of Peace

There are numerous reasons why sleep eludes us, many of which we cannot do much about. But sometimes unwanted wakefulness is caused by anxious thoughts, worry, or guilt. It is then that the example of David in Psalm 4 can help.

•   He called out to God, asking for mercy and for God to hear his prayer *(4:1)*

•   He also reminded himself that the Lord does hear Him when He calls on Him *(4:3)*

•   David encourages us "meditate within your heart on your bed, and be still" *(4:4)*

•   Focusing our minds on the goodness, mercy, and love of God for His word, our loved ones and ourselves can aid us in trusting the Lord *(4:5)*

•   The Lord desires to help us set aside our worries about finding solutions to our problems and place our trust in Him to work things out. He can "put gladness" in our hearts
 (4:7) So that we might "lie down in peace and sleep; for you alone, O Lord, make us dwell in safety." *(4:8)*

Give me a Spirit of peace, Dear Lord, midst the storms and the tempests that roll, that I may find rest and quiet within a calm buried deep in my soul.

> *"If we want to discover God's best for our life, we must trust that His way is better than our plans and desires. No one understands our needs better than He does. Our Father sees what lies ahead and knows what He wants to accomplish in every situation."*
>
> *Dr. Charles Stanley*

Chapter 16

"Therefore. Being justified by faith, we have peace with God through our Lord Jesus Christ."

(Roman 5:1)

Firm Foundation

The two-sided reality of the Christian life is on one hand, we are complete in Christ (our acceptance with him is secure). On the other hand, we are growing in Christ (we are becoming more and more like him). At one and the same time, we have the status of Kings and the duties of Slaves. We feel both the presence of Christ and the pressure of sin.

We enjoy the peace that comes from being made right with God, but we still face daily problems that often help us grow. If we remember these two sides of the Christian life, we will not grow discouraged as we face temptations and problems. Instead, we will learn to depend on the power available to us from Christ who lives in us by the Holy Spirit.

No matter how much life changes, we can have hope, for we are anchored to a firm foundation that will never be shaken *(Isaiah 8:16)*.

The believer's hope rests in the Triune God - Father, Son, and Holy Spirit. Our heavenly Father knows each of us by name *(Isaiah 43:1)*. Our Savior keeps every divine promise *(2Corinthians 1:20)* and the Holy Spirit assures us that we are secure.

Chapter 17

"And the Lord said unto Gideon, by the three hundred men that lapped will I save you and deliver the Midianites into thine hand: and let all the other people go every man unto his place."

(Judges 7:7)

Be strong in the Lord

God had Gideon use 300 men, horns, jars, and blazing torches against armies that were "as numerous as locusts; and their camels were without number" *(Verse 12).* It was impossible for they had neither the manpower nor the military hardware. They had one thing that worked for them and that was all they needed. They had God's promise. "With these 300 men I will rescue you and give you victory" *(Verse 7).*

Are you facing a formidable challenge? The Lord has said "Behold, I am the Lord, the God of all flesh...... Is there anything too hard for me?" *(Jeremiah 32:27)*

Song writer: Linda Lee Johnson

"Be strong in the Lord and be of good courage; your mighty Defender is always the same. Mount up with wings, as the eagle ascending; Victory is sure when you call on His name."

With God, all things are possible.

Chapter 18

"And the King of Israel said unto Jehoshaphat, I will disguise myself and will go to the battle: but put thou on thy robes. So, the King of Israel disguised himself, and they went to the battle."

(2 Chronicles 18:29)

Call upon God

Jehoshaphat's troubles began when he joined forces with the evil King Ahab. Almost at once he found himself the target for soldiers who mistakenly identified him as Ahab. He could have accepted this fate because he deserved it, but instead he cried out to God, who miraculously saved him.

When we sin and the inevitable consequences follow, we may be tempted to give up. *"I chose to sin; I may think it's my fault and I must accept the consequences."* While we may deserve what comes to us, that is no reason to avoid calling on God for urgent help. Had Jehoshaphat given up, he might have died. No matter how greatly you have sinned, you can still call upon God.

Chapter 19

"And said, O Lord God of our fathers, art not thou God in heaven? And rulest not thou over all the kingdoms of the heathen? And in thine hand is there not power and might, so that none is able to withstand thee?"

(2 Chronicles 20:6)

God's help when we face struggles

Jehoshaphat's prayer had several essential ingredients:

- He committed the situation to God, acknowledging that only God could save the nation

- He sought God's favor because his people were God's people

- He acknowledged God's sovereignty over the current situation

- He praised God's glory and took comfort in His promises

- He professed complete dependence on God for deliverance, not on himself. To be God's kind of leader today, follow Jehoshaphat's example – focus entirely on God's power rather than your own.

Verse 15

As the enemy bore down on Judah, God spoke through Jahaziel, "Do

not be afraid or discouraged....for the battle is not yours, but God's." We may not fight an enemy army, but every day we battle temptation, pressure, and "rulers…. of the dark world" *(Ephesians 6:12)* who want us to rebel against God. Remember, as believers, we have God's Spirit in us. If we ask for God's help when we face struggles, God will fight for us. And God always triumphs.

How do we let God fight for us!

- By realizing the battle is not ours, but God's

- By recognizing human limitations and allowing God's strength to work through our fears and weaknesses.

- By making sure we are pursuing God's interests and not just our own selfish desires

By asking God for help in our daily battles.

> *"Then Eliezer the son of Dodavah of Mareshah prophesied against Jehoshaphat, saying, because thou hast joined thyself with Ahaziah, the Lord hath broken thy works. And the ships were broken, that they were not able to go to Tarshish." (2 Chronicles 20:37)*

Verse 37

Jehoshaphat met disaster when he joined forces with wicked King Ahaziah. He did not learn from his disastrous alliance with Ahab **(18:28-34)** or from his father's alliance with Aram **(16:2-9)**. The partnership stood on unequal footing because one man served the Lord and other worshipped idols. We encounter disaster when we enter into partnership with unbelievers because our very foundations differ *(2 Corinthians 6:14-18)* while one serves the Lord the other does not recognize God's authority.

Inevitably, the one who serves God is faced with the temptation to compromise values. When that happens, spiritual disaster results. Before entering into partnerships, ask:

- What are my motives?

- What problems am I avoiding by seeking this partnership?

- Is this partnership the best solution, or is it only a quick solution to my problems?

- Have I prayed or asked others to pray for guidance?

- Are my partner and I really working toward the same goals?

- Am I willing to settle for less financial gain in order to do what God wants?

Chapter 20

*"Behold, I am the Lord, the God of all flesh; is there
anything too hard for me?"*

(Jeremiah 32:27)

God sees our situation

Trust does not come easy. It was not easy for Jeremiah to publicly
buy land already captured by the enemy, but he trusted God.

It was not easy for David to believe that he would become King,
even after he was anointed, but he trusted God *(1 Samuel 16:31)*.

It was not easy for Moses to believe that he and his people would
escape Egypt, even after God spoke to him from a burning bush, but
he trusted God *(Exodus 3:1-4; 20)*.

It is not easy for us to believe that God can fulfill his impossible
promises either, but we must trust him. God, who worked in the lives
of Biblical heroes will work in our lives too if we will let him.

After Jeremiah bought the field, he began to wonder if such a move
was wise. He sought relief in prayer from his nagging doubts. In this
prayer, Jeremiah affirmed that God is creator and Redeemer, the wise
judge of all the ways of the people. God loves us and sees our situation.
Whenever we doubt God's wisdom or wonder if it is practical to obey
him, we can review what we already know about him. Such thoughts
and prayers will quiet our doubts and calm our fears.

Chapter 21

"The Lord God is my strength, and he will make my feet like hinds 'feet, and he will make me to walk upon my high places. To the chief singer on my stringed instruments."

(Habakkuk 3:19)

Habakkuk's Struggle

When Habakkuk was troubled, he bought his concerns directly to God. After receiving God's answers, he responded with a prayer of faith. Habakkuk's example is one that should encourage us as we struggle to move from doubt to faith. We do not have to be afraid to ask questions of God. The problem is not with God and his ways but with our limited understanding of him.

When circumstances around us become almost unbearable, we wonder if God has forgotten us. But remember He is in control. God has a plan and will judge evildoers in His time. If we are truly humble, we will be willing to accept God's answers and await His timing.

Struggle and Doubt – Habakkuk asked God why the wicked in Judah were not being punished for their sin. He could not understand why a just God would allow such evil to exist. God promised to use the Babylonians to punish Judah. When Habakkuk cried out for answers in his time of struggles, God answered him with words of hope.

God wants us to come to him with our struggles and doubts. His answers may not be what we expect, however, God sustains us by revealing himself to us. Trusting him leads to quiet hope, not bitter resignation.

God's Sovereignty – Habakkuk asked God why he would use the wicked Babylonians to punish his people. God said that He would also punish the Babylonians after they had fulfilled His purpose. God is still in control of this world despite the apparent triumph of evil. God does not overlook sin. One day He will rule the whole earth with perfect justice.

Hope – God is the Creator, He is all-powerful. He has a plan, and He will carry it out. He will punish sin. He is our strength and our place of safety. We can have confidence that He will love us and guard our relationship with Him forever. Hope means going beyond our unpleasant daily experiences to the joy of knowing God. We live by trusting in Him, not by the benefits, happiness, or success we may experience in this life. Our hope comes from God.

God's answer to Habakkuk is the same answer He would give us. "Be patient! I will work out my plans in my perfect timing." It is not easy to be patient, but it helps to remember that God hates sin even more than we do.

To trust God fully is to trust Him even when we do not understand why events occur as they do. Christians must trust that God is directing all things according to His purposes. Habakkuk praised God for answering His questions. Evil will not triumph forever. God is in control, and He can be completely trusted to vindicate those who are faithful to Him. We must patiently wait for Him to act.

Habakkuk affirmed that even in the times of starvation and loss, He would still rejoice in the Lord. When nothing makes sense, and when troubles seem more than you can bear, remember that God gives strength. Take your eyes off your difficulties and look to God. God is alive and in control of the world and its events. We cannot see all that God is doing and we cannot see all that God will do. But we can be assured that He is God and will do what is right. Knowing this can give us confidence and hope in a confusing world.

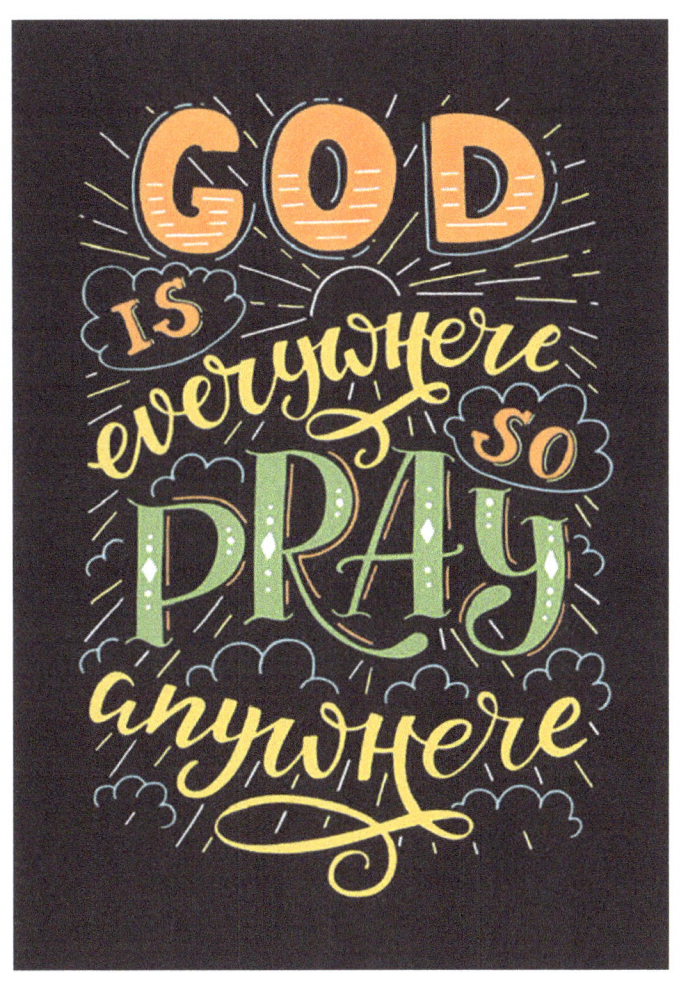

Chapter 22

"Now when Daniel knew that the writing was signed, he went into his house: and his windows being open in his chambers toward Jerusalem, he kneeled upon his knees three times a day, and prayed, and gave thanks before his God, as he did aforetime."

(Daniel 6;10)

Our Disciplined Prayer life

Daniel was working with those who did not believe in His God, but he worked more efficiently and capably than all the rest. He attracted the attention of the pagan king and earned a place of respect. One of the best ways to influence non-Christian employers is to work diligently and responsibly. How well do you represent God to your employer?

Daniel made enemies at work by doing a good job. Perhaps you have had a similar experience. When you begin to excel you will find that co-workers may look for ways to hold you back and tear you down. How should you deal with those who would cheer at your downfall and even try to hasten it?

Conduct your whole life above reproach. Then you will have nothing to hide, and your enemies will have a difficult time finding legitimate charges against you. Of course, this will not always save you from attacks and like Daniel you will have to rely on God for protection. God is in control fighting this battle for you.

Daniel stood alone. Although he knew about the law against praying to anyone except the King, he continued to pray three times a day as he always had. Daniel had a disciplined prayer life. Our prayers are usually interrupted not by threats, but simply by the pressure of our schedules. Do not let threats or pressures cut into your prayer time. Pray regularly, no matter what, your prayer is your lifeline to God.

Daniel made no attempt to hide his daily prayer routine from his enemies. Hiding would have demonstrated that he was afraid of the other government officials. Daniel continued to pray because he could not look to the King for the guidance and strength that he needed during this difficult time. Only God could provide what He really needed. The person who trusts in God and obeys His will is untouchable until God takes him or her. To trust God is to have immeasurable peace. God who delivered Daniel will deliver you. Do you trust him with your life? Evil deeds often backfire on those who plan cruelty.

Chapter 23

*"Those who hope in the Lord will renew their strength.
They will soar on wings like eagles. They will run and
not grow weary; they will walk and not faint."*

(Isaiah 40:31)

When We Feel Burned Out

1) God does not become weary or tired.

2) He gives strength to the weary and power to those who are not mighty.

3) The next time you feel too tired or frustrated to go on, remember this; Our God is not exhaustible.

Even the strongest people get tired at times, but God's power and strength never diminish. He is never too tired or too busy to help and listen, His strength is our source of strength. When you feel all of life crushing down on you and you cannot take another step, remember that you can call upon God to renew your strength.

Hoping in the Lord is expecting that his promise of strength will help us to rise above life's distractions and difficulties. Do you believe God loves you and wants the best for you? Can you relax, confident that his purposes are right? Are you convinced that he has the power to control all of life and your life as well? Though your faith may be struggling or weak, accept his provisions and his care for you.

Chapter 24

"That Christ may dwell in your hearts by faith: that ye, being rooted and grounded in love....and to know this love that surpasses knowledge-that you may be filled to the measure of all the fullness of God."

(Ephesians 3:17,19)

God's Love

God's love is total – it reaches every corner of our experience; God's love is wide – it covers the breath of our own experience, and it reaches out to the whole world. God's love is long – it continues the length of our lives; God's love is high – it rises to the heights of our celebration and elation; God's love is deep – it reaches to the depth of discouragement, despair, and even death.

When you feel shut out or isolated, remember that you can never be lost to God's love. In union with Christ and through his empowering Spirit, we are complete. We have all the fullness of God available to us. But we must appropriate that fullness through faith and through prayer as we live our daily lives for Him. You can ask the Holy Spirit to fill every aspect of your life to the fullest.

Chapter 25

"With all lowliness and meekness, with longsuffering, forbearing one another in love."

(Ephesians 4:2)

Be Gentle with Each Other

Believers are to live with gentleness. Being gentle is part of the Fruit of the Spirit *(Galatians 5:3)* and important in the life of every believer. Believers are to exhibit patience. Patience is another part of the Fruit of the Spirit *(Galatians 5:23)* and a necessity if we are going to show love to others. Believers are to live with love towards one another.

No one is ever going to be perfect here on earth so we must accept and love other Christian despite their faults. When we see faults in fellow believers, we should be patient and gentle. Is there someone whose actions or personality really annoys you? Rather than dwelling on that person's weaknesses or looking for faults, pray for him or her, then do even more – spend time together and see if you can learn to like him or her.

Chapter 26

"Be ye angry, and sin not: let not the sun go down upon your wrath, neither give place to the devil."

(Ephesians 4:26-27)

Do Not Nurse Your Anger

Paul's warning is a little different than could be expected, however, he does not say "don't be angry." Rather, he says "be angry." There are things that can certainly be angering in today's culture. It is a matter of fact that if you love certain things, then you will be angry at certain other things.

For example, if you love God and His name, then you will be angry when others seek to misrepresent and mischaracterize Him. With any amount of heart in your chest, you will certainly feel love and reciprocal anger. This kind of anger is righteous, and it is this righteous anger that Paul commands you to have if you have been converted.

But there is a type of anger that should not be found in any Christian. It is the type of anger that springs from sin and causes sin. Therefore, Paul says, "Be angry, and sin not" *(Ephesians 4:26)*. Many times, anger does not find its moorings in righteousness but in sinfulness. When someone says wrong things about us (or true bad things) and we respond in anger, it is typically not because we are such lovers of truth. Rather, it is because they have challenged our self-image and self-worth, and in pride we think we are so far above their lowly claims. In pride, we respond through sinful wrath.

This type of anger is rooted in the sin of pride and is wrong. It starts with sin, and typically ends in another kind of sin (violence, revenge…). If we have been converted, we do not respond in this way. If the sin of our hearts draws us towards disobedience, we must remember that Christ has changed us, and we must fight with everything in us while relying on Christ's strength to offer us help in our struggle.

This cleansing and getting right should be a rapid thing. We must not hesitate and allow anger and sin to linger. Paul says it this way, "let not the sun go down" without getting it right. This means that it is never okay to be angry at another and not to seek reconciliation. Jesus made this point of the necessity of immediate reconciliation in both **Matthew 5** and **Matthew 18**, telling his followers to go immediately to those with whom you have problems.

The Bible does not tell us that we should not feel angry, but it points out that it is important to handle our anger properly. If bottled up inside, it can cause us to become bitter and destroy us from within. Paul tells us to deal with our anger immediately in a way that builds relationships rather than destroys them. If we nurse our anger, we will give Satan an opportunity to divide us. Do not let the day end before you begin to work on mending your relationship

Chapter 27

"Who leave the paths of uprightness, to walk in the ways of darkness."

(Proverbs 2:13)

Learn from your mistakes

It is human nature to hide our sins or overlook our mistakes. But it is hard to learn from a mistake you do not acknowledge making. What good is a mistake if it does not teach you something? To learn from an error, you need to admit it, confess it, analyze it, and adjust so that it does not happen again. Everybody makes mistakes, only fools repeat them.

Chapter 28

"Cast not away therefore your confidence, which hath great recompence of reward."

(Hebrews 10:35)

Stand Firm

The Bible gives us a clear choice between two life directions. Because life often forks off in two directions, you must take the higher road, even though it looks more difficult and treacherous. That road gets steep in places. The climb takes a toll on your energy, it gets lonely and slippery because Satan blows ice on the narrow passages.

Despite its danger, the higher road is bound for the peak, and you will make it – God has a lifetime around you. When you are tempted to falter in your faith or to turn back from following Christ, keep focused on what he has done for you and what he offers in the future, then keep climbing.

When you are pressured to give up and turn your back on Christ, remember the benefits of standing firm and continuing to live for Christ.

Chapter 29

"But let patience have her perfect work, that ye may be perfect and entire, wanting nothing."

(James 1:4)

Be Patient

Instead of complaining about our struggles, we should see them as opportunities for growth. Thank God for promising to be with you in rough times. Ask Him to help you solve your problems or to give you the strength to endure them. Then be patient, God will not leave you alone with your problem, He will stay close and help you grow.

Chapter 30

"And she said unto them, call me not Naomi, call me Mara; for the Almighty hath dealt very bitterly with me."

(Ruth 1:20)

Resist Bitterness

Ruth loves her mother-in-law, Naomi. Recently widowed, Ruth begged to stay with Naomi wherever she went, even though it would mean leaving her homeland, ending her plea with, "your people will be my people and your God my God" *(Ruth 1:16)*.00

Ruth's faithfulness to Naomi as a daughter-in-law and friend is a great example of love and loyalty. Ruth, Naomi, and Boaz are also faithful to God and his laws. Ruth showed great kindness to Naomi. In turn, Boaz showed kindness to Ruth.

When you face bitter times, God welcomes your honest prayers, but be careful not to overlook the love, strength, and resources that He provides in your present relationships. Do not allow bitterness and disappointment to blind you to your opportunities.

Chapter 31

"For our God is a consuming fire."

(Hebrews 12:29)

"For our God is a consuming fire."

There is a big difference between the flame of a candle and the roaring blast of a forest fire. We cannot even stand near a raging fire even with sophisticated firefighting equipment, a consuming fire is often beyond human control.

God is not within our control either; we cannot force him to do anything for us through our prayers. He cannot be contained. Yet He is a God of compassion; He has saved us from sin, and He will save us from death. But everything that is worthless and sinful will be consumed by the fire of His wrath. Only what is good, dedicated to God and righteous will remain.

Chapter 32

"Wherein in time past ye walked according to the course of this world, according to the prince of the power of the air, the spirit that now worketh in the children of disobedience."

(Ephesians 2:2)

Gratitude to Christ

Paul reminded me that I was once dead in my transgressions and sins, in which I used to live when I followed the ways of this world and of the ruler of the Kingdom of the air, the Spirit who is now at work in those who are disobedient.

Christ has set me free from the bondage of sin. We must never forget our past, the condition from which Jesus saved us. Those memories are the best fuel for our gratitude to Christ for all He has done in our behalf.

Chapter 33

"The eyes of the Lord range throughout the earth to strengthen those whose hearts are fully committed to him."

(2 Chronicles 16:1-9)

The Eyes of the Lord

Both Judah and Israel suffered from faithless forgetfulness. Although God has delivered them even when they were outnumbered, they repeatedly sought help from pagan nations rather than from God. With help from God alone, Asa had defeated the Cushites in open battle. But his confidence in God had slipped, and now he sought only a human solution to his problem.

It is not a sin to use human means to solve our problems, but it is a sin to trust them more than God, to think they are better than God's ways, or to leave God completely out of the problem-solving process. Asa's problem was that he completely ignored God's help.

As we face our own battles and challenges, let us remember that God is our best ally. He strengthens us when we are willing to "serve up" a whole-hearted commitment to Him.

Chapter 34

"If it be so, our God whom we serve is able to deliver us from the burning fiery furnace, and he will deliver us out of thine hand, O King."

(Daniel 3:17)

God's Presence

King Nebuchadnezzar enforced his threat, sending Daniel's friends into the furnace. They acted on the truth of God's Word, and Jesus walked with them through their trial *(Daniel 3:25)*. Because of the way they handled their situation, the King marveled at God's power to keep the three men safe from the flames. God is glorified when we stand against sin and temptation.

They trusted God to deliver them, but they were determined to be faithful regardless of the consequences. If God always rescued those who were true to him, Christians would not need faith. Their religion would be a great insurance policy and there would be lines of selfish people ready to sign up. We should be faithful to serve God whether he intervenes on our behalf or not. Our eternal reward is worth any suffering we may have to endure first.

When my situation feels unbearable, God's constant presence comforts me. He strengthens me and reassures me of His unchanging goodness, limitless, power, and sustaining grace. And when I am tempted to doubt my Lord, I am encouraged by the determined faith of Shadrach, Meshach, and Abednego. They worshiped God and trusted He was with them even when their situation seemed hopeless.

Chapter 35

"And God spoke unto Moses, and said unto him, I am the Lord, and I appeared unto Abraham, unto Isaac, and unto Jacob, by the name of God Almighty, but by my name JEHOVAH was I not known to them."

(Exodus 6:2-3)

God is working on our behalf

Small problems need only small answers, but when we face great problems, God has an opportunity to exercise his great power. Big problems put you in perfect position to watch God give big answers. When God redeems us from sin he delivers us, accepts us, and becomes our God. Then he leads us to a new life as we follow him.

Sometimes a clear message from God is followed by a period when no change in the situation is apparent. During that time, seeing setbacks may turn people away from wanting to hear more about God. If you are a leader, don't give up. Keep bringing people God's message as Moses did. By focusing on God who must be obeyed rather than on the results to be achieved, good leaders see beyond temporary setbacks and reversals.

There are times in our lives when we face the storms of life: marriage, wayward child, financial problems, sickness, hurt, loss of a loved one and the list goes on and on. We feel as if God has given up on us but I am here to tell you God has not given upon us. Sometimes God sends us a clear message which is followed by a period when no change in the situation is apparent.

There are times when our hurts and fears, storms of life can close our ears to the hopeful Words of God. But the Lord does not stop speaking to us when it is hard for us to hear. He continues working on our behalf just as He did in delivering His people from Egypt. Even when we do not sense God's presence, His loving care is all around us.

About the Author

Vivienne Caldwell, a native from Kingston, Jamaica W.I., born to Enid and Martin Clarke. She has two children, one son, Andrew Caldwell, one daughter, Jerri-Lee Caldwell, and five grandchildren. She migrated to the United Stated in 1985 for a better life.

Vivienne Caldwell lives in Queens, NY, a believer in Christ who gave her life to Christ in March 1979. Before she started writing, Vivienne got a graduate degree in Public Administration, Credentials in Health Care Management. She has been working in Corporate America for over 30 years and 6 years as a supervisor. Vivienne Caldwell is also a Licensed Real Estate Agent and owns her own Loan Signing and fingerprinting business.

There are circumstances in our life that we would love to change if we could. We all go through hardship or unfulfilled desire, do not look at your circumstances but look to the Lord for strength, only God can strengthen us when we fully submit ourselves to Him. **Be Strong!**

www.ingramcontent.com/pod-product-compliance
Lightning Source LLC
Chambersburg PA
CBHW051334120626
46547CB00016B/2538